BUSES, COACHES & TROLLE[YBUS]
Recollections

C000156298

SCOTLAND 1963 and 1964

Henry Conn

Contents

Acknowledgements

Introduction

Introduction	2
Inverness and North East Scotland	3
Aberdeen	9
Dundee and Fife	14
Edinburgh and district	22
Glasgow and district	30
Strathclyde and South West Scotland	54
1963 No 1 Records	16
1964 No 1 Records	50, 51
1963 Happenings	38, 41
1964 Happenings	47, 51, 62, 63
1963 Arrivals & Departures	53
1964 Arrivals & Departures	53
Index to operators and vehicles	64

© Henry Conn 2016

ISBN 978 1 85794 486 0

All rights reserved. No part of this publication may be reproduced, stored in a retrieval system or transmitted, in any form or by any means, electronic, mechanical, photocopying, recording or otherwise, without prior permission in writing from Silver Link Publishing Ltd.

First published in 2016

British Library Cataloguing in Publication Data

A catalogue record for this book is available from the British Library.

My most sincere thanks go to Tony Belton, whose magnificent colour views of Glasgow are seen in this book (further volumes covering the years 1962 through to 1966 will feature much more of Tony's wonderful photography). All the other pictures are from my own collection, the vast majority of which are photographs by Stewart Brown, from whom I acquired the negatives – many thanks.

Title page: **GLASGOW** The last 90 trolleybuses to be delivered to Glasgow Corporation, Nos TB35 to TB124, were 8-foot-wide two-axle vehicles unique to Glasgow, and were the mainstay of routes 105, 106 and 107. Arriving at Clarkston terminus on 25 September 1964 is No TB65 (FYS 826), a Crossley-bodied BUT 9613T that entered service on 1 February 1958 and was in service on the last day of trolleybuses in Glasgow, 27 May 1967. Note the Western SMT Leyland PD3 in the background. *Tony Belton*

Silver Link Publishing Ltd
The Trundle
Ringstead Road
Great Addington
Kettering
Northants NN14 4BW

Tel/Fax: 01536 330588
email: sales@nostalgiacollection.com
Website: www.nostalgiacollection.com
Printed and bound in the Czech Republic

The PSV Circle fleet histories and issues of *Buses Illustrated* for both years were sources of information for this volume.

The biggest news from 1963 was the assassination of US President Kennedy on 22 November, which thrust Lyndon B. Johnson into the role of President and led to the murder two days later of Lee Harvey Oswald by nightclub owner Jack Ruby. This was a difficult time to become President, with mounting troubles in Vietnam where the Viet Cong guerrillas had now killed 80 American Advisers. Meanwhile the continued campaign for civil rights by the black community caused violent reactions from whites in Mississippi, Virginia and Alabama, where the black civil rights leader Martin Luther King Jr was arrested (1963 was the year of his 'I have a dream' speech).

Films released in 1963 included *The Birds*, *The Great Escape*, *Cleopatra*, *The Longest Day*, *Lawrence of Arabia*, *Mutiny on the Bounty* and *To Kill a Mockingbird*. Popular TV programmes *The Virginian* and *Lassie* were first aired. Ladies' fashion clothes and hairstyles included fur boots and towering hairdos for evening wear. The iconic rock band the Beatles recorded their very first full-length album during February of 1963 – the entire album was recorded in one day. It carried the title *Please Please Me* after their single, and featured a mix of original songs by Paul McCartney and John Lennon and popular covers. Some of the most popular tracks from the album included *I Saw Her Standing There*, *Love Me Do*, and *Twist and Shout*. It was released in March 1963 and topped the charts in the United Kingdom for 30 weeks until was replaced by another Beatles album, *With The Beatles*. The average house price in the UK was £3,160, and a new Ford Cortina was £675.

In 1964 the US Congress authorised war against North Vietnam, and more American servicemen were dying. Following the murder of three civil rights workers in Mississippi, the President signed the Civil Rights Act of 1964, but this did not stop the violence, which continued to increase in many American cities. Lyndon B. Johnson was also returned to power after a landslide victory. This was also the year that the Beatles took the world and America by storm, and Beatlemania went into overdrive as the group released a series of No 1 hits, including *I Want To Hold Your Hand* and *All My Loving*. Other British groups also found success, including the Rolling Stones and the Animals, and together with the American talent of the Supremes and Bob Dylan, many say that this was one of the greatest years for music in the last century. *Top of the Pops* premiered in 1964. In sport, a young, loud and talented boxer by the name of Cassius Clay won the World Heavyweight boxing championship from Sonny Liston. The year also saw the abolition of the death penalty in the UK, Malta gaining independence from the UK, the commencement of work on the Aswan Dam to divert the River Nile, the first Ford Mustang rolling off the production line, and the most powerful earthquake in US history, at 9.2 on the Richter scale, striking South Alaska. Nelson Mandela was sentenced to life imprisonment, Elizabeth Taylor married Richard Burton (for the first time), the Great Train Robbers received 30 years each, the Summer Olympics were held in Tokyo, and the Winter Olympics in Innsbruck, Austria. Films premiered this year were *The Carpetbaggers*, *It's a Mad Mad Mad Mad World*, *My Fair Lady* and *Mary Poppins*. Actors born in 1964 were Keanu Reeves and Russell Crowe.

Enjoy the nostalgia…

THURSO This is Highland No E6 (HGC 148), a Guy Arab II that had been new to London Transport as No G369 in September 1945 with utility Weymann bodywork. The bus was acquired by Western SMT in December 1951 and was fitted with a new Alexander body in November 1952. Highland acquired it in May 1963, and immediately before its departure it was fitted with platform doors. It then spent most of its service outstationed at Thurso for Dounreay workers' transport. This view was taken on 30 July 1963.

On this day it was reported from Dounreay that the maximum power output achieved was 60 megawatts thermal, corresponding to an electrical output of 14.2 megawatts. This was the highest heat level at which a fast breeder reactor had operated anywhere in the world. The average electrical output of the reactor was 2.75 million units per month.

Photo **DESTINATIONS**

1   **GLASGOW** (Title page)

Inverness and North East Scotland

2   **THURSO** (Previous page)

3   **HELMSDALE**

4   **DINGWALL**

5   **INVERNESS**

6   **INVERNESS**

7   **INVERNESS**

8   **INVERNESS**

9   **ROSEHEARTY**

Aberdeen

10   **ABERDEEN**

11   **ABERDEEN**

12   **ABERDEEN**

13   **ABERDEEN**

14   **ABERDEEN**

15   **ABERDEEN**

16   **ABERDEEN**

17   **ABERDEEN**

18   **ABERDEEN**

19   **ABERDEEN**

HELMSDALE Standing in front of The Bridge Hotel in Helmsdale, Sutherland, is Midland No MPD 247 (VWG 386), an Alexander-bodied Leyland PSUC1/2 new in May 1963. This view is dated 31 August 1964, and MPD 247 would survive until sold for scrap in February 1979.

DINGWALL The Highland Transport Company purchased new eight Guy Arab IIs between June and December 1946. Nos 35 to 38 (BST 277/278/325/326) had Strachan bodywork, and Nos 47, 50, 51 and 52 (BST 570/573/570/571) had NCME bodywork, and all were transferred to Highland Omnibuses on 11 February 1952. On a local service in Dingwall on 5 May 1963 is No E37 (BST 325); it would be withdrawn and scrapped in 1965.

Four months before this view was taken, the Beatles played at Dingwall Town Hall to an audience of 19. Apparently they were late in arriving, and when they went on stage one by one they were wearing leather jackets, jeans, long scarves and winkle-pickers. Within a year of that gig they were the most popular band in the world.

INVERNESS During May 1963 Highland acquired 12 ECW-bodied Bristol LD6Gs from Scottish Omnibuses, numbered L1 to L12 (NSG 780 to 791). Working a local Inverness service to Kessock Ferry on 10 September 1963 is No L1 (NSG 780); this bus would return to Scottish Omnibuses in October 1971, remaining there until July 1975, when it was sold for scrap.

Right: **INVERNESS** Highland No E72 (EST 392), a Guy Arab III with rare full-fronted Strachan bodywork, is seen leaving Farraline Park bus station on a schools service. This bus was exhibited at the 1950 Commercial Motor Show and entered service with Highland Transport in May the following year. It later passed to James Peace of Kirkwall in 1970 as the first of only two double-deckers ever to operate on Orkney. This view was taken on 30 September 1964, and the other bus in view is No B53 (HWS 933), an Alexander-bodied AEC Regal IV new in June 1951 and acquired from Western SMT in 1964.

Left: **INVERNESS** Between June and December 1962 Highland acquired from Scottish Omnibuses five Duple coach-bodied AEC Regals. which had been new in 1946. Representative of these on 3 January 1963 is No B44 (ESC 452). Dating from November 1946, it was withdrawn and sold in 1965.

That night the Beatles opened their 1963 tour with a performance in Elgin.

INVERNESS Northern acquired the substantial business of James Sutherland of Peterhead in March 1950. One of the buses acquired was No NPA 198 (EAV 459), a very smart-looking Duple coach-bodied Leyland PS1 new in March 1948. This view was taken 10 August 1963.

The No 1 single on this day was Sweets for my Sweet *by the Searchers.*

ROSEHEARTY is 4 miles west of Fraserburgh, and heading there on 20 August 1964 is Northern No NRA 59 (BWG 104), an Alexander-bodied Leyland PD1 new in September 1948. This bus was sold for scrap in October 1970.

Aberdeen

Left: **ABERDEEN** This is Aberdeen No 142 (BRG 935), a Duple-bodied Daimler CWA6 new in June 1944, in Guild Street on 16 May 1964. It was delivered with slatted seats, which were replaced by upholstered seats in 1949; rubber-mounted windows were fitted by the Corporation during 1957-59, and the bus remained on fleet strength until September 1965, a remarkably long service life for a wartime utility-bodied bus.

Above: **ABERDEEN** Seen on the same day exiting King Street at Castle Street is No 148 (BRS 30), a Duple-bodied Daimler CWA6, new in June 1945. When delivered this bus had upholstered seats and additional opening windows, and was later fitted with rubber-mounted windows by the Corporation some time between 1957 and 1960.

Just two days later there was an outbreak of typhoid in the city, and eventually more than 500 cases were diagnosed, with patients quarantined at the City Hospital in Urquhart Road. It was eventually traced to contaminated Fray Bentos tinned corned beef from South America, sold in the city's branch of the Scottish grocery chain William Low. Pollution from the waters of the Uruguay River appears to have been the source of the contamination, which probably entered a defective tin through a small puncture. The infected meat then contaminated a meat-slicing machine within the William Low shop, leading to the spread of the disease. Happily no fatalities resulted.

Right: **ABERDEEN** This is No 27 (BRS 527), one of a batch of five Weymann-bodied AEC Regent IIIs that had been new in June 1947, each costing £3,304. This example, photographed on 31 July 1964, would be sold for scrap in September 1967.

By this date no new typhoid cases had been diagnosed in Aberdeen.

Left: **ABERDEEN** Standing in the new Guild Street bus station on 10 September 1963 is former James Sutherland coach No NA 94 (DSA 113), a Brush coach-bodied AEC Regal new in August 1947; it would return to its home depot of Peterhead soon after this view was taken.

The Beatles tour of 1963 visited the Beach Ballroom in Aberdeen on 6 January 1963. Tickets cost 3 shillings and the group received £45 for their appearance. They would never return to the city.

Left: **ABERDEEN** Strachans (Deeside Omnibus Service) ran two services, one travelling the South Deeside Road from Aberdeen to Banchory, then via Ballater to Braemar on the North Road, the other going from Banchory to Ballater via Ballogie. The company used a stance at Bon Accord Street in Aberdeen, and seen there on 1 May 1963 is No 27 (FAV 333), a Roberts-bodied Foden PVSC6 new in July 1949.

Above: **ABERDEEN** On the same May day in Bon Accord Street is Strachans No 2 (GCA 54), a Bellhouse Hartwell-bodied Foden PVSC6 new to Jones & Sons of Ruabon in September 1949; it passed to Strachans in September 1959.

Three weeks later, on 24 May, the fine old Aberdeenshire house at Seaton was destroyed by fire. A Georgian mansion in the Classic Renaissance style, designed by James Gibbs in 1725, it had been built from hand-made bricks.

Left: **ABERDEEN** Also working to Aberdeen on that day was Strachans (Deeside Omnibus Service) No 9 (SUG 7), which was the company's newest bus at the time this photograph view was taken; it had been acquired from Wallace Arnold of Leeds the month before. Deeside would be acquired by Northern on 3 May 1965 and No 9, as Northern No NAC 51, would be the last Deeside bus to survive, being sold in April 1973. Alongside is Deeside No 4 (EYS 222), a Plaxton-bodied Foden PVSC6 new to Campbell of Aberdeen in June 1947 and passed to Deeside in August 1957.

Left: **ABERDEEN** Heading for Heatheryfold on route 17 is Aberdeen No 186 (GRG 186), one of a batch of 20 Crossley-bodied Daimler CVG6s new in 1954, purchased for tram replacement. This view was taken on 10 July 1964; behind the bus is a statue of William Wallace by William Grant Stevenson, erected in 1888 opposite His Majesty's Theatre and across from Union Terrace Gardens. No 186 would be sold for scrap in April 1971.

Right: **ABERDEEN** No 241 (KRG 241) was one of the large number of buses purchased new for tram replacement; it is an MCCW-bodied Daimler CVG6 new in 1957, and cost £4,882. This view, with the whole length of Union Street in the background, was taken on 15 September 1964; the south side of Union Street Bridge was widened during that year when a row of shops were added.

ABERDEEN In Holburn Street on 1 September 1964 is No 260 (KRS 260), a Metro-Cammell-bodied AEC Regent V new in May 1958. It would pass to Grampian Regional Transport in May 1975, but with large numbers of new Leyland AN68s arriving early the following year, No 260 would be sold for scrap in January 1976.

Photo **DESTINATIONS**

Dundee and Fife

20	**DUNDEE**
21	**DUNDEE**
22	**DUNDEE**
23	**DUNDEE**
24	**DUNDEE**
25	**DUNDEE**
26	**BLAIRGOWRIE**
27	**ARBROATH**
28	**METHIL**
29	**LOCHGELLY**
30	**DUNFERMLINE**
31	**DUNFERMLINE**
32	**KIRKCALDY**

Dundee and Fife

DUNDEE Seen in the early afternoon of 27 August 1963, this is Dundee Corporation No 5 (YJ 9635), a Weymann-bodied Daimler CVD6 that had been delivered in November 1947; it would be sold to a dealer in 1965.

In this month Dundee Corporation increased its bus fares due to a deficit of £50,000.

DUNDEE After the Second World War Barnards Ltd were all tooled up but, after industrious wartime activity, the order books were empty. The company therefore diversified into a three-year burst of bus and coach bodybuilding; having no previous experience of coachwork, two managers from Northern Coachbuilders of Newcastle, Horace Hatton and Jack Herdman, joined the company in 1948 to head up the new Barnards business. In the three years 1948-50, Barnards made a total of 115 bus and coach bodies, among them 37 double-deckers. Dundee purchased new ten Barnard-bodied Daimler CVD6s in 1949, and in 1950 a further nine AEC Regent IIIs with Barnard bodies were delivered. Representing the latter batch is No 150 (AYJ 368), heading for Ninewells on 1 September 1963. No 150 remained in the fleet until sold for scrap in 1970.

1963
No 1 Records

January
Cliff Richard   *The Next Time/Bachelor Boy*
Shadows   *Dance On*
Jet Harris and Tony Meehan   *Diamonds*

February
Frank Ifield   *The Wayward Wind*

March
Cliff Richard   *Summer Holiday*
Shadows   *Foot Tapper*

April
Gerry and the Pacemakers   *How Do You Do It?*

May
Beatles   *From Me To You*

June
Gerry and the Pacemakers   *I Like It*

July
Frank Ifield   *Confessin' (That I Love You)*

August
Elvis Presley   *(You're The) Devil In Disguise*
Searchers   *Sweets For My Sweet*
Billy J Kramer and the Dakotas   *Bad To Me*

September
Beatles   *She Loves You*

October
Brian Poole and the Tremeloes   *Do You Love Me*

November
Gerry and the Pacemakers   *You'll Never Walk Alone*

December
Beatles   *I Want To Hold Your Hand*

DUNDEE No 182 (ETS 962) was one of 35 MCCW-bodied Daimler CVG6s purchased new by Dundee for tram replacement in 1955. On the left of this view, dated 3 August 1964, is a Watson's Tours Ford coach, RTS 461, which was registered on 20 March 1964.

Left: **DUNDEE** Exiting Seagate on the same day is No 216 (JXC 218), a Cravens-bodied AEC Regent III that had entered service with London Transport at its Mortlake depot in June 1949. Between an overhaul in August 1953 and August 1955 it worked out of Middle Row, Stockwell and East Grinstead depots before being sold to Birds in July 1956. In all, Dundee acquired from Birds 30 Cravens-bodied AEC Regent IIIs for tram replacement, reportedly for £1,750 each. No 216 would be sold to Docherty of Monifieth in August 1968.

Right: **DUNDEE** took delivery of 20 Alexander-bodied Daimler CRG6LXs, Nos 80 to 99 (AYJ 80B to 99B). This view of No 88 (AYJ 88B) was taken on 1 September 1964 – note that it has a conductor.

The No 1 single on this day was Have I the Right? *by the Honeycombs, and the No 1 album was* A Hard Day's Night *by the Beatles.*

Below: **BLAIRGOWRIE** During 1952 A. & C. McLennan purchased EES 468, a Leyland PSU1/15 that was bodied in-house by the company. On 23 April 1964 the bus is working to Kirkmichael, which is north-west of Blairgowrie. This bus had a long service life with McLennan, not being withdrawn and sold for scrap until May 1973. The bus on the left is GDK 301, which was new to Yelloway of Rochdale in June 1948, and passed to McLennan in 1958; it was sold on to Duncan of Kinloch Rannoch in 1959, but reacquired by McLennan in February 1963. McLennan fitted it with a new body for one-person operation with a cut-away cab; this was the last new body built by McLennan, and the bus was still licensed in November 1977.

Above: **DUNDEE** Built on Forfar Road in the Stobswell region of the city, the Maryfield tram depot was opened by Dundee Corporation in 1901; its red and blue brick and curvilinear gables are features that the building still retains to this day. Originally constructed to hold a dozen trams, it was later extended to house up to 70. Using a Standard track gauge, remnants of the tram network can also still be seen throughout the city, including in the pedestrianised areas of Murraygate. In its glory years in the 1930s, Dundee Corporation had approximately 100 trams on the streets, in their distinctive green and cream finish. But by the immediate post-war era the city's transport network was in desperate need of modification; after abandonment of the tram service on 27 October 1956 and the subsequent burning of the vehicles, the Corporation's diesel bus fleet was stored in Maryfield from the 1960s onwards. Standing in Maryfield depot, with tram track still visible on 1 August 1964, is No 63 (YJ 9136), an MCCW-bodied AEC Regent III new in 1948; it would have a long service life before being withdrawn in February 1968 to be used by the Corporation Building Department.

ARBROATH During December 1949 MCCW-bodied BMMO S10 No 3580 (NHA 580) entered service with Midland Red. When it was withdrawn in June 1962, T. D. Alexander Greyhound acquired it and used it as a showroom in Arbroath from the following month. This view was taken on 20 April 1963.

Cinema-goers this month would be watching Hitchcock's The Birds.

Left: **METHIL** When Walter Alexander & Sons Limited was split up on 15 May 1961, Fife received a large number of all-Guy Arab IIIs, all but one dating from 1948. This is No FG 89 (BMS 859), which was new in March 1948 and after 18 years of service was sold for scrap in November 1966. This view was taken on 22 April 1963; the depot code is AL, indicating that FG 89 was allocated to Aberhill depot, Methil, in service to Buckhaven.

Right: **LOCHGELLY** Also following the Walter Alexander split Fife received five Alexander coach-bodied Albion MR11Ls, Nos FNL 10 to 14 (KWG 585 to 589). Allocated to Lochgelly depot was No FNL 10 (KWG 585), and this view was taken in Lochgelly on 20 July 1963 with the bus in service to Cupar, 23 miles away.

Built in this year in Cupar was St Columba's Roman Catholic Church, by Peter Whiston. It is a circular, harled building with a distinctive Scottish slate roof and chimney spire.

Below: **DUNFERMLINE** Standing in the town's bus station on 30 April 1963 is No RD 159 (7407 SP), an ECW-bodied Bristol FLF6G new in June 1962. Beside it is No PA 24 (AWG 559), an Alexander-bodied Leyland PS1 new in May 1947. Furthest from the camera is No PD 57 (GWG 283), an Alexander-bodied Leyland PSUC1/2, new in November 1955.

During April 1963 local boys the Shadettes made the first of many appearances at the Kinema Ballroom; they would later become Nazareth in February 1970.

Above: **DUNFERMLINE** When the split of Walter Alexander & Sons Ltd took place on 15 May 1961 the new Fife company received 516 of the company's 1,937 bus fleet. They remained in the blue and cream livery of Alexander's; the only change was the addition of the word 'Fife'. From 1962 Fife adopted an Ayres red and cream livery, and the fleet comprised mainly Guy and Leyland vehicles. Fife had acquired a total of five Guy Arab IIs from the business of W. Greig of Inverness in October 1947, and this is No FRO 574 (CST 5) at Carnegie Street bus stance in Dunfermline on 10 January 1963. This bus was ordered by Greig, but was not delivered until the takeover, and remained in the fleet until sold for scrap in November 1966.

Left: **KIRKCALDY** Working a Kirkcaldy local town service on 5 January 1963 is No RD 89 (MMS 741), an ECW-bodied Bristol LD6G new in March 1959.

On 6 October 1963 the Beatles played two 30-minute shows at the Carlton Theatre in Kirkcaldy; tickets cost 15 shillings and songs performed included Do You Want to Know a Secret, I Saw Her Standing There, Love Me Do, From Me to You, Please Please Me *and* Twist and Shout.

Photo	**DESTINATIONS**
	Edinburgh and district
33	**EDINBURGH**
34	**EDINBURGH**
35	**EDINBURGH**
36	**EDINBURGH**
37	**EDINBURGH**
38	**EDINBURGH**
39	**EDINBURGH**
40	**EDINBURGH**
41	**EDINBURGH**
42	**EDINBURGH**
43	**EDINBURGH**
44	**EDINBURGH**
45	**EDINBURGH**
46	**EDINBURGH**
47	**EDINBURGH**
48	**DUNBAR**
49	**BATHGATE**
50	**BATHGATE**
51	**BATHGATE**
52	**FALKIRK**
53	**GRANGEMOUTH**

Edinburgh and district

EDINBURGH This is Albion LR1 Lowlander 747 EUS, the third chassis built, the second LR1, and Albion's demonstrator. During is demonstration period it spent long spells on loan to Glasgow Corporation and Edinburgh Corporation, then after it had finished demonstrating it entered service with the Preston-area independent Bamber Bridge Motor Services, retaining its Albion grille badge. This view was taken on 25 March 1963. Because of its proximity to Central Depot, the 19 route saw a mix of buses, including demonstrators.

The Traverse Theatre in Edinburgh was founded in 1963; during the 1960s Richard Wilson was a regular performer and in the 1970s Timothy Dalton, Billy Connolly, Robbie Coltrane, Simon Callow and Steven Berkoff all performed there.

EDINBURGH Leaving St Andrew Square bus station on 18 May 1963 is DSG 176, with stickers showing that it is on hire to Scottish Omnibuses Limited, with the destinations of Easthouses and Newtongrange. This bus was new to Scottish Motor Traction in April 1943 as its No E1; it was sold to Highland Omnibuses in January 1959, reacquired by SOL in May 1963, and sold for scrap a short time after this view was taken.

On this day in Edinburgh Helen Shapiro was appearing at the ABC Regal in Lothian Road.

EDINBURGH On the same day, standing in the bus station are DWS 352, an NCME-bodied Guy Arab II new in August 1943, and beyond it DWS 845, a Roe-bodied Guy Arab II new in May 1944. DWS 352 was acquired by Highland Omnibuses in December 1955 and the other bus in July 1955. Their service life with SOL was very short.

Above: **EDINBURGH** Leaving the bus station and heading for Glenrothes, also on 29 April 1964, is Fife No FGA 3 (GMS 413), an Alexander coach-bodied Guy Arab LUF 6HLW that had been new in May 1955; it would be scrapped by Fife in November 1970. The Edinburgh Corporation bus working service 11 is No 783 (OFS 783), an MCCW-bodied Leyland PD2/20 new in June 1957.

Above: **EDINBURGH** Two Park Royal-bodied AEC Monocoaches, FMS 977 and FMS 983, new to W. Alexander & Sons in November 1954, were acquired by SOL in May 1960. Allocated to Broxburn depot, this is No B 38 (FMS 983) leaving St Andrew Square bus station in service to Oakbank on 29 April 1964.

That night the Beatles were in concert at the ABC Cinema in Lothian Road. The Fab Four revisited the ABC and Edinburgh for the final time in October 1964.

Right: **EDINBURGH** Parked in the bus station on 20 September 1963 is No B 348 (GSC 236), a Burlingham-bodied AEC Regal III new in October 1948; at the time of this view it was allocated to Musselburgh depot, and would sold to a dealer a few weeks later. This batch of 19 Regal IIIs had 7.7-litre engines with crash gearboxes and featured side-facing seats over the rear wheel arches.

Left: **EDINBURGH** Between September and December 1949 20 lowheight AEC Regent IIIs with Duple 8-foot-wide bodies were delivered, and representing this batch is No BB 77 (GSF 660), allocated to Broxburn and heading for Blackridge in West Lothian on 21 September 1963. These Regent IIIs did not have a central cream band, but rather aluminium ribbing; I still find the Burlingham-bodied Regents an attractive bus, and all had been sold by the end of 1966.

The No 1 single this day was She Loves You *by The Beatles – are you singing this song now?*

Below left: **EDINBURGH** Twenty Burlingham coach-bodied AEC Regal IIIs were also delivered in 1949, and one of them was No B 378 (GSF 697), seen here standing in the parking area of St Andrew Square bus station, below the bus stances. They were allocated throughout the SOL operating area, and when this view was taken on 4 September 1964 No B 378 was allocated to Galashiels depot.

On this day the Forth Road Bridge was opened the Queen; the toll was 2s 6d for cars.

Below: **EDINBURGH** During January and February 1952 10 Alexander coach-bodied AEC Regal IVs were delivered, numbered B 445 to B 454 (JSF 145 to 154). By the time this view was taken on 30 October 1964 this coach, No B 445, had been downgraded to bus duties in Lothian Green livery.

On this day Sandie Shaw, the barefooted girl from Dagenham, was at No 1 with the Burt Bacharach/Hal Prince single (There's) Always Something There to Remind Me.

Left: **EDINBURGH** During June 1958 Walter Alexander took delivery of No AC 145 (KWG 569), an Alexander coach-bodied AEC Reliance, and new to Baxter's in November 1958 was SVD 113, ex-Scottish Omnibuses, an Alexander-bodied Leyland PSUC1/2. These two buses were exchanged in April 1963, and No AC 145 became Scottish Omnibuses No B 35, and it is seen here leaving St Andrew bus station for North Berwick on 4 May 1964. On the right is one of the ECW coach-bodied Bristol LS6Gs, about to depart on a Glasgow express service.

Below left: **EDINBURGH** Working route 8 to Gilmerton on 20 September 1964 is Edinburgh Corporation No 962 (OFS 962), an Alexander-bodied Guy Arab IV new in October 1956; the Arabs were quite commonly operated on routes 8, 14 and 19. They were of the same vintage as the Orion-bodied Leyland PD2/20s, but all had been withdrawn by 1972. No 962 was withdrawn in late 1969 and sold for scrap in January 1970.

Below: **EDINBURGH** On 1 December 1962 Baxter's of Airdrie was acquired by Scottish Omnibuses, with a fleet comprising 52 vehicles – 25 double-deckers, 23 single-deck buses and four coaches. Of the double-deck buses, 22 were Leylands; the other three were AECs, and two of which were Regent Vs with Massey bodywork new in December 1957. Both were quickly transferred from Airdrie to Edinburgh, and here we see No BB 19 (PVD 567) on 19 September 1964.

Right: **EDINBURGH** The Corporation's first Leyland PD3, No 998, was an Alexander-bodied PD3/2 that featured a unique Homalloy front. It was exhibited at the 1957 Scottish Motor Show and went out on loan to Central SMT and Western SMT in 1958 before going to Edinburgh in November of that year. This view of the bus working the Circle service 19 was taken on 22 September 1964; it passed to Highland Omnibuses in March 1974 and was sold to Avro, Corringham, in December 1976 via the dealer Ensign.

On this day Hunterston A nuclear power station opened.

Below: **EDINBURGH** From September 1960 through to January 1961 Edinburgh Corporation took delivery of 50 Weymann-bodied Leyland PSUC1/3s, Nos 51 to 100 (VSC 51 to 100). Photographed on the Royal Mile while working service 46 to Tollcross on 20 September 1964 is No 80 (VSC 80).

Right: **EDINBURGH** During late 1947 and through to March 1948 Scottish Omnibuses took delivery of 40 Alexander-bodied AEC Regent IIIs. In St Andrew Square bus station on 1 October 1964, about to work to Rosewell, is No BB 22 (ESC 422). All 40 had long service lives, and No BB 22 was exported to the USA in February 1969.

Above: **DUNBAR** The fleet of Stark's of Dunbar was acquired by Scottish Omnibuses on 1 January 1964, and comprised 14 single-deckers. One of the coaches was Scottish Omnibuses No H 4 (SS 8015), a Leyland PSU1/15 with the classic Burlingham Seagull coachwork, new in October 1951. This view was taken on 5 May 1964; sadly the coach was sold for scrap in December 1966.

Above: **BATHGATE** When Baxter's of Airdrie was acquired by Scottish Omnibuses, the company had one Daimler CRG6LX on order, with Alexander D-style bodywork. This bus, No DD 961 (9961 SF), was delivered directly to SO in October 1963 and it is seen here in Bathgate on 25 October 1963 working the trunk service 310 between Glasgow and Edinburgh. The bus was transferred to Baxter's in 1964 and repainted in Baxter's livery, but was burned out in May 1965 and received a new Alexander body, becoming a one-person bus at that time.

Left: **BATHGATE** No BB 962 (9962 SF), a Park Royal-bodied AEC Bridgemaster, was originally ordered by Baxter's as its No 80 (480 DVA), but it was re-registered and repainted before entry into service. In this view, it retains Baxter's non-standard destination box – a hexagonal one was later fitted. The location is the Scottish Omnibuses depot in Bathgate on 1 July 1964. Also identified in this view are, on the extreme left, No B702 (SWS 702), a Park Royal coach-bodied AEC Reliance; then No B453 (JSF 153), an Alexander-bodied AEC Regal IV demoted to bus duties; and next but one a very new Alexander-bodied AEC Reliance of the AFS B batch. On the right is light-green-liveried ECW-bodied Bristol LD6G No AA 758 (USC 758), which was new in January 1960.

BATHGATE Working the Grangemouth to Bathgate service on 2 February 1963 is No AB1 (BMS 110), a Burlingham-bodied AEC Regal III new in November 1947; it would be scrapped by Alexander in July 1965.

A month earlier, on 1 January 1963, the Forth & Clyde Canal was officially closed for navigation.

FALKIRK Standing in Falkirk bus station on a service to Stirling on 25 April 1963 is No MPD 265 (SVD 113), an Alexander coach-bodied Leyland PSUC1/2 new to Baxter's of Airdrie in November 1958 and acquired by Alexander in December 1962; it would be sold for scrap in November 1974.

On this day, David Moyes, footballer and manager was born in Glasgow.

GRANGEMOUTH Between January 1963 and January 1964 Alexander took delivery of 44 Alexander-bodied Albion LR1s, Nos MRE 1 to 44, and working a Grangemouth local service on 15 October 1964 is No MRE 31 (VWG 369), which was new in October 1963.

On this day a UK General Election was held and Labour defeated Sir Alec Douglas-Home's Conservatives.

Photo	**DESTINATIONS**

Glasgow and district

53 CUMBERNAULD
54 GLASGOW
55 GLASGOW
56 GLASGOW
57 GLASGOW
58 GLASGOW
59 GLASGOW
60 GLASGOW
61 GLASGOW
62 GLASGOW
63 GLASGOW

Glasgow and district

CUMBERNAULD In service to Bo'ness on 31 August 1963 is No MRB 258 (RMS 690), an Alexander-bodied Leyland PD3/3C new in March 1961; this bus was part of a batch of 17 constructed from Leyland PS1 chassis and fitted with Leyland OPS2/1 engines. All were withdrawn between December 1975 and August 1976.

GLASGOW The first single-deck trolleybus for Glasgow Corporation, No TB 35 (FYS 765), a Weymann-bodied BUT RETB1, was exhibited at the Earls Court Motor Show in September 1950; it was then demonstrated at Atherton in March 1951 and Edinburgh in June 1951. As No TBS 1, it was rebuilt to front entrance only in August 1961, and is seen here working route 101 on 14 May 1964; it was sold for scrap in April 1965.
Tony Belton

On this day a by-election at Rutherglen was a gain by Labour from the Conservatives.

GLASGOW At Glasgow Cross working route 102 to Polmadie on 7 November 1963 is No TBS 8 (FYS 772), an East Lancashire dual-doorway-bodied BUT RETB1 that entered service on 1 July 1953. It was rebuilt to centre-entrance in November 1960 and was withdrawn from service on 14 November 1964. *Tony Belton*

On this day the Kinross and West Perthshire by-election took place and the Conservatives retained the seat.

Left: **GLASGOW** On 20 June 1964 this is No TBS 20 (FYS 995), a Burlingham-bodied BUT RETB1 that had entered service on 1 December 1958. This batch of unique trolleybuses, TBS 12 to 21, ran exclusively on the suburban route 108 between Ballogie Road and Paisley Road Toll. The final day of operations for one of them, No TBS 21, was 3 March 1967, after which it was acquired for preservation. *Tony Belton*

Above: **GLASGOW** Heading for the most southerly terminus of Glasgow's trolleybus routes is No TG 16 (FYS 791), a Weymann-bodied Sunbeam F4 that had entered service on 1 August 1953. It would operate for the last time on 27 February 1965 and was sold for scrap in June of that year. *Tony Belton*

Left: **GLASGOW** Passing the Empire Theatre on 10 February 1963 is No TG 5 (FYS 780), an Alexander-bodied Sunbeam F4 that entered service on 1 August 1953. The final curtain came down on the Empire Theatre on 31 March that year, with a cast that included Iain Cuthbertson, Albert Finney, Ricki Fulton and Andy Stewart. The last day of operation for No TG 5 was 27 February 1965, and it was sold for scrap four months later. *Tony Belton*

GLASGOW
Leaving the
Shawfield terminus
of route 101 for
Cathedral Street
on 7 March 1964
is TB 8 (FYS 708),
an MCCW-bodied
BUT 9641T that
entered service on
25 March 1949 and
was last in service
on 29 April 1966.
Tony Belton

*Born on this day in
Glasgow was Tommy
Sheridan, socialist
politician and MSP.*

GLASGOW Heading for Muirend on route 105 on 21 July 1964 is No TB 16 (FYS 716), an MCCW-bodied BUT 9641T that entered service on 1 May 1949 and was last used in service on 20 April 1966. *Tony Belton*

On this day, while sheltering under a tree at Crews Hill golf course in Enfield, John White, aged just 27, was killed by a lightning strike.

Above: **GLASGOW** In Jura Street on route 106 to Riddrie on 13 April 1963 is No TB 52 (FYS 813), a Crossley-bodied BUT 9613T that entered service on 1 June 1958 and operated until 4 March 1967. *Tony Belton*

On this day footballer Maurice Johnston was born in Glasgow.

Right: **GLASGOW** Also in Jura Street on the same day is No TB 95 (FYS 856), a Crossley-bodied BUT 9613T that entered service on 1 June 1958 and was last in service on 1 October 1966. *Tony Belton*

GLASGOW Seen on 21 July 1964, working route 107 in Clarkston Road, this is No TB 39 (FYS 800), a Crossley-bodied BUT 9613T that entered service on 24 July 1957. After just nine years in service, this trolleybus was sold for scrap in August 1966. *Tony Belton*

DESTINATIONS

Glasgow and district
(continued)

54	**CUMBERNAULD**
55	**GLASGOW**
56	**GLASGOW**
57	**GLASGOW**
58	**GLASGOW**
59	**GLASGOW**
60	**GLASGOW**
61	**GLASGOW**
62	**GLASGOW**
63	**GLASGOW**
64	**GLASGOW**
65	**GLASGOW**
66	**GLASGOW**
67	**GLASGOW**
68	**GLASGOW**
69	**GLASGOW**
70	**GLASGOW**
71	**Nr BALFRON**
72	**PAISLEY**

1963 Happenings (1)

January
England suffers the coldest winter since 1740
Hugh Gaitskell, leader of the Labour Party dies
General De Gaulle vetoes UK entry into the
    Common Market (EEC)

February
Harold Wilson becomes leader of the Labour Party

March
Publication of the infamous 'Beeching Report' on the
    future of British Railways

April
Princess Alexandra marries Angus Ogilvy at
    Westminster Abbey

June
Pope John XXIII dies, and Pope Paul VI is instituted
John Profumo, Secretary of State for War, resigns
    over his affair with Christine Keeler

August
UK, US and Russia sign a partial nuclear test ban
    treaty in Moscow
£2.5 million is stolen from a Glasgow-London mail
    train in Buckinghamshire in the 'Great Train
    Robbery'
Dr Martin Luther King makes his 'I have a dream'
    speech in Washington

GLASGOW This is the one and only Daimler CRG6LX with Alexander bodywork in the Glasgow Corporation fleet. No D268 (SGD 730) is seen here under trolleybus wires in Renfield Street on route 61 on 1 December 1963. This bus had been new in May of that year, and was used as a Daimler demonstrator visiting Bournemouth and Southampton in July.

Above: **GLASGOW** Working route 24 on 2 February 1963 is
No LS12 (FYS 683), a Glasgow Corporation Leyland RT3/1 built on Weymann
frames, which was new in January 1957. A total of 30 of these vehicles were
built with Leyland 0680 engines and pneumocyclic gearboxes, and were, when
new, front entrance and centre exit; No LS12 was rebuilt in September 1961, as
seen in this view. These buses were used mainly on lowbridge routes 24 and 30;
with a running time of less than 10 minutes, route 24 must have been a pretty
boring service. Note the Vauxhall Victor estate, originally registered in Inverness.

Above right: **GLASGOW** Heading for Larkfield depot is No D66 (FYS 494),
new in February 1951. Originally bodied by Mann Egerton, it received the
Alexander body from No D60 in July 1960. This view was taken on 23 October
1964, and less than a year later No D66 was sold for scrap.

Right: **GLASGOW** During March 1955 Walter Alexander took delivery of 20
ECW-bodied Bristol LS6Gs, which were to be the only bus-bodied LS6Gs to
run in Scotland. All 20 were transferred to Fife in May 1961 and this is No FE 3
(FWG 838), which at the time this view was taken at Buchanan Street depot on
20 April 1964, was allocated to Cupar depot.

On this day Peter and Gordon were at No 1 with World Without Love.

GLASGOW Alexander relieved congestion at the Buchanan Street site in 1944 by building Dundas Street bus station, an open-air terminal close by on the south-eastern corner of Dundas Street/Killermont Street and Parliamentary Road crossroads; both bus stations were next door to the warehouses of Buchanan Street railway goods station. Arriving at Dundas Street on 1 October 1963 is No A73 (BMS 107), a Burlingham-bodied AEC Regal new in 1947; it was sold to a showman in July 1965. Behind it is No MRB 179 (KWG 640), an Alexander-bodied Leyland PD3/3 new in March 1958.

1963 Happenings (2)

September
Christine Keeler is arrested for perjury, and the Denning Report on the 'Profumo affair' is published
Fylingdales early warning station comes into operation

October
Harold Macmillan resigns as Prime Minister and is succeeded by Sir Alec Douglas-Home

November
Dartford Tunnel opens
US President John F. Kennedy assassinated; Lyndon B. Johnson becomes US President

December
Greek liner *Lakonia* sinks 250 miles west of Gibraltar while on a Christmas cruise

GLASGOW In March 1949 Alexander took delivery of five Burlingham coach-bodied Daimler CVD6s, Nos D31 to D35 (BWG 570 to 574). In Dundas Street on 26 October 1963 is the now renumbered MD 34 (BWG 573), and behind it one of Scottish Omnibuses' batch of 20 Park Royal-bodied Leyland PD2/20s, which were new in February and March 1957. They were originally allocated to Airdrie and moved to Baillieston depot when it opened in 1960.

The Scottish League Cup Final was played on this day, Rangers beating Greenock Morton 5-0.

Above: **GLASGOW** In Buchanan Street heading for Lesmahagow on 25 July 1964 is Central SMT No L438 (DVD 296), an all-Leyland PD2/1 that was new in 1948 and was sold for scrap in June 1968. In the 1960s the George Hotel, behind the bus, was owned by Peter Fox, and has more recently been host to *Taggart*, and scenes from films including *Trainspotting*, *Small Faces* and *Carla's Song*. The elusive millionaire steadfastly refused to sell or refurbish the George, a dilapidated Victorian pile, with funereal wood panelling and imitation art deco, despite constant threats of compulsory purchase orders from Glasgow City Council and offers of multi-million pound corporate deals – until 1997, that is, when he netted £30 million by selling to the retail property developer Helical.

Above: **GLASGOW** In the parking area on 2 May 1963, with the warehouses of Buchanan Street goods station in the background, is No PC 17 (CMS 383), an Alexander-bodied Leyland PSU1/15 new in May 1952.

On this day the Rootes car factory opened at Linwood, Renfrewshire, to produce the Hillman Imp. Linwood closed in 1981, leaving mass unemployment in the area.

Right: **GLASGOW** Exiting Dundas Street in the winter sunshine of 10 December 1964 is Fife No FPD 48 (GWG 274), an Alexander-bodied Leyland PSUC1/2 new in November 1955. In the right background is a brand-new Glasgow Corporation Alexander-bodied Leyland PDR1/1. No FPD 48 is showing allocation to Cupar depot, and its destination of Ceres is a small village 2 miles from Cupar and 7 miles from St Andrews.

Far left top: **GLASGOW** Also making its way out of Dundas Street bus station, on 3 March 1963, is No N2 (JMS 389), an Alexander coach-bodied Albion Nimbus MR9L new to Alexander in 1957. This model was 24 feet long and 8 feet wide and had a Leyland four-cylinder 3.83-litre engine and a four-speed Albion gearbox. No N2 was sold to dealer in December 1968 and purchased by Bickers of Coddenham in February 1969, but unfortunately was involved in an accident a month later and subsequently sold for spares.

Left: **GLASGOW** This is the Western SMT St Enoch air terminal for coaches to Glasgow Airport. St Enoch railway station is in the background; opened in 1876, it was operational until 27 June 1966, when it was closed as part of the rationalisation of the railway system by Beeching. This view of Western SMT No 1908 (AAG 101B) was taken on 14 October 1964.

Far left bottom: **GLASGOW** On the same day and in the same location is BOAC No 0214F (RAG 652), a Harrington Crusader-bodied Ford 568E, one of the small fleet of coaches that BOAC used between Glasgow and Prestwick.

Left: **GLASGOW** The North British Railway's station in the city was Queen Street, where it opened its own self-named hotel, forming the backdrop to this photograph. A total of 30 Albion Lowlanders were purchased new by Central SMT, and this is No A19 (FGM 19), an Alexander-bodied LR1 new in 1963 and seen here on 3 July 1964. Central sold all its Lowlanders in 1965, with Alexander Fife taking 18 and Highland Omnibuses 12, including No A19, and it would remain in the Highland fleet until sold to Omnibus Promotions by July 1979.

Above: **GLASGOW** With a very healthy load of passengers for Paisley North on 31 May 1964, Western SMT Lowlander No 1878 (VCS 432) is an Alexander-bodied Albion LR1 that was new in 1963; it makes an interesting comparison with the lowheight Leyland PD3 behind, which has a side gangway on the upper deck whereas the Lowlander does not.

On this day Billy Davies, football player and manager, was born in Glasgow.

Left: **GLASGOW** Working service 13 to Greenfield is Glasgow Corporation No L319 (SGD 321), an Alexander-bodied Leyland PD2/24 new in May 1960 and photographed on 1 February 1963. During that month a 36-hour blizzard caused heavy drifting in most parts of the UK, with drifts reaching 20 feet and winds up to 80 miles per hour.

Below: **GLASGOW** Also working service 13 to Greenfield, but on a sunnier 10 November 1964, is No L398 (SGD 400), the only Alexander-bodied Leyland PD3A/2 in the Glasgow Corporation fleet. Exhibited at the 1960 Commercial Motor Show, No L398 had a St Helen's-style front (the only one in the fleet), fluorescent lighting and a non-standard laminate interior trim.

1964 Happenings (1)

January

Leyland Motors announces supply of 450 buses to Cuba

Pope Paul VI visits Jerusalem

John Glenn enters politics

France and China establish diplomatic relations

February

Beatles visit New York and appear on *The Ed Sullivan Show*

Leaning Tower of Pisa in danger of falling – Italian Government launches appeal to help stabilise structure

March

Malta gains independence

Coronation of King Constantine II of Greece

Jack Ruby found guilty of murdering Lee Harvey Oswald, assassin of President John F. Kennedy

European Space Agency established

Anchorage (USA) and surrounding area suffer major earthquake

Radio Caroline (North) starts pirate radio transmission from ship anchored off Ramsey, Isle of Man

April

Beatles take top five slots in Billboard Singles chart

Ford of America unveils Mustang to the public – the legend begins!

Launch of BBC2

Tanzania formed by merger of Tanganyika and Zanzibar

Above: **GLASGOW** Entering Dundas Street bus station on 20 April 1963 is RO 451 (WG 9980), a Guy Arab II originally bodied by Roe and new in November 1943; a new ECW body was fitted in July 1951. This bus operated with the Lawson fleet from new until May 1961; withdrawn from passenger service in 1965, it became a tree-lopper in October 1965 until sold for scrap in February 1969.

Above right: **NEAR BALFRON** With the hills and mountains of Loch Lomond in the background, working from the Midland depot of Balfron on 24 June 1964 is No MAC 73 (GWG 477), an Alexander-bodied AEC Monocoach new in July 1955. This bus would be acquired by Highland Omnibuses in December 1970 and remain with that company until 1973.

On this day in Dundee, the athlete Liz McColgan was born.

Above: **PAISLEY** The first bus service operated by McGill's Bus Service Ltd of Barrhead was introduced between Barrhead and Paisley in 1933, and double-deck buses were introduced in 1939. In 1949 McGill's purchased a new all-Leyland PD2/1, EHS 113, seen here in Paisley on 21 October 1964.

Photo DESTINATIONS

Glasgow and district
(continued)

73 **PAISLEY**

74 **BARRHEAD**

75 **PAISLEY**

76 **PAISLEY**

77 **Nr NEWTON MEARNS**

78 **BRIDGE OF WEIR**

Top right: **PAISLEY** Also photographed on that day was McGill's VKV 99, a Willowbrook-bodied Daimler CVG6-30 new in 1958 and acquired in 1961.

Right: **BARRHEAD** Standing in McGill's Barrhead depot on 5 June 1964 are NHS 764, a Massey-bodied Leyland PD2/20 new in 1959, and beyond it OHS 979, a Daimler CVG6 also with a Massey body and also new in 1959.

On this day an explosion at the Paisley animal feed plant of Brown & Polson took place at 6.40am. Workers who had arrived for the 6.45am shift had to run for their lives, but sadly four men were killed and four badly injured.

1964
No 1 Records (1)

January
Beatles — *I Want To Hold Your Hand*
Dave Clark Five — *Glad All Over*
Searchers — *Needles and Pins*

February
Bachelors — *Diane*
Cilla Black — *Anyone Who Had a Heart*

March
Billy J. Kramer and the Dakotas — *Little Children*

April
Beatles — *Can't Buy Me Love*
Peter and Gordon — *A World Without Love*

May
Searchers — *Don't Throw Your Love Away*
Four Pennies — *Juliet*
Cilla Black — *You're My World*

June
Roy Orbison — *It's Over*

July
Animals — *The House of the Rising Sun*
Rolling Stones — *It's All Over Now*
Beatles — *A Hard Days Night*

August
Manfred Mann — *Doo Wah Diddy Diddy*
Honeycombs — *Have I the Right?*

September
Kinks — *You Really Got Me*
Herman's Hermits — *I'm Into Something Good*

October
Roy Orbison — *Oh, Pretty Woman*
Sandie Shaw — *(There's) Always Something There To Remind Me*

PAISLEY Between November 1951 and March 1952 Western SMT took delivery of seven Alexander lowheight-bodied Daimler CVG6s, Nos 940 to 946 (BSD 289 to 295). Working a local Paisley service out of Johnstone depot on 3 September 1963 is the first of them.

PAISLEY At the same location on that day is No 1016 (ESD 217), an NCME lowheight-bodied Guy Arab III new in 1953. It was withdrawn from service late in 1967, and acquired by Blair & Palmer of Carlisle in March 1968.

1964
No 1 Records (2)

November
Supremes   *Baby Love*

December
Rolling Stones   *Little Red Rooster*
Beatles   *I Feel Fine*

1964
Happenings (2)

May
Habitat launched by Terence Conran
More than 300 killed and 480 injured as football fans riot at Peru versus Argentina match in Lima

June
Nelson Mandela jailed after receiving life sentence from South African court
US Senator Edward Kennedy suffers serious injuries in plane crash; pilot killed

July
Serious escalation in Vietnam War as US death toll passes 400
US sends 5,000 more troops to Vietnam, bringing total deployed to 21,000
Malawi declares independence from Britain
At Wimbledon Roy Emerson beats Fred Stolle to win Men's Singles Final, and Maria Bueno beats Margaret Smith to win Women's Singles Final
Donald Campbell sets record of 690.91kmph (429.31mph) for turbine vehicle

Left: **NEAR NEWTON MEARNS** This is Western SMT No 1703 (TCS 151), an Alexander-bodied Albion LR1. The first of this model to be produced, it was exhibited at the 1961 Scottish Motor Show at Kelvin Hall, then toured England and Wales on a demonstration tour on trade plates. It entered service with Western SMT in May 1962 and is seen here working out of the Newton Mearns depot to Mearnskirk on 14 November 1963; it was sold to Highland Omnibuses in May 1966. Of the 274 Albion Lowlanders produced, Western SMT would purchase new 111.

Above: **BRIDGE OF WEIR** During 1951 Ribble purchased Nos 781 to 900, all-Leyland PSU1/15s; they carried the first coach bodywork built by Leyland since pre-war days, they were of all-metal construction, and were air-conditioned. They began to be withdrawn from service as early as 1962, with the last surviving until 1966, many having found new owners. This is one of them, ECK 148, which was acquired by Garner's Buses of Bridge of Weir in May 1963 and entered service in September 1963. This view was taken on 20 April 1964; the bus was withdrawn by Garner's in late 1966 and was last licensed by Hughes of Armadale in November 1967.

1963 Arrivals & Departures

Births

James May	Journalist	16 January
Ian Cook	Footballer	18 January
Andrew Ridgeley	Musician	26 January
George Monbiot	Journalist	27 January
Martin Bashir	Journalist	29 January
Jerome Flynn	Actor	16 March
David Thewlis	Actor	20 March
Julian Lennon	Musician	8 April
Natasha Richardson	Actress	11 May
Jason Isaacs	Actor	6 June
George Michael	Musician	25 June
Tracey Emin	Artist	3 July
Fatboy Slim (Norman Cook)	Musician	31 July
Tamsin Archer	Musician	3 August
Jarvis Cocker	Musician	19 September
Rick Allen	Musician	1 November
Lena Zavaroni (d.1999)	Musician	4 November
Nicolette Sheridan	Actress	21 November
Eddie 'The Eagle' Edwards	Ski-jumper	5 December

Deaths

Edward Titchmarsh	Mathematician	(b.1899)	18 January
Hugh Gaitskell	Politician	(b.1906)	18 January
J. C. Powys	Writer	(b.1872)	17 June
Guy Burgess	Double agent	(b.1911)	30 August
Peter Craven	Motorcycle racer	(b.1934)	20 September
Aldous Huxley	Writer	(b.1894)	22 November
C. S. Lewis	Writer	(b.1898)	22 November
John F. Kennedy	US President	(b.1917)	22 November

1964 Arrivals & Departures

Births

Nicolas Cage	Actor	7 January
Bridget Fonda	Actress 27 January	
Christopher Eccleston	Actor	16 February
Matt Dillon	Actor	18 February
Juliette Binoche	Actress	9 March
Prince Edward		10 March
Shane Richie	Actor	10 March
Martin Donnelly	Racing driver	26 March
Russell Crowe	Actor	7 April
Adrian Moorhouse	Swimmer	24 May
Kathy Burke	Actress and comedienne	13 June
Johnny Herbert	Racing driver	25 June
Bonnie Langford	Actress	22 July
Sandra Bullock	Actress	26 July
Jim Corr	Singer/musician	31 July
Keanu Reeves	Actor	2 September

Deaths

Alan Ladd	Actor	(b.1913)	29 January
Peter Lorre	Actor	(b.1904)	23 March
Jawaharlal Nehru	Indian PM	(b.1889)	27 May
Jim Reeves	Singer	(b.1923)	31 July
Sean O'Casey	Writer	(b.1880)	18 September
Harpo Marx	Comic actor	(b.1888)	28 September
Cole Porter	Composer	(b.1891)	15 October
Herbert Hoover	31st US President	(b.1874)	29 October
Sam Cooke	Singer	(b.1931)	11 December

Photo DESTINATIONS

Strathclyde and South West Scotland

79 SALTCOATS

80 SALTCOATS

81 MILLPORT

82 ISLE OF ARRAN

83 ISLE OF ARRAN

84 LOCHGILPHEAD

85 TARBERT

86 CAMPBELTOWN

87 SOUTHEND

88 MACHRIHANISH

89 BALLOCK

90 WISHAW

91 En route to GLASGOW

92 Nr MOTHERWELL

93 LANARK

Strathclyde and South West Scotland

SALTCOATS Clyde Coast Services Limited were the smallest of the associations of Ayrshire bus operators and operated the large Saltcoats route. New in September 1956 was this Beadle-bodied Commer TS3, XKT 784, which was purchased by Hutchinson's Coaches of Overtown in September 1957. By December 1961 it had been sold to Millburn Motors Limited, and later that month it passed to D. D. & G. McGregor, a member of Clyde Coast Services Limited. In June 1964 it moved again to W. J. Shields, another Clyde Coast member, with whom it remained until sold by December 1970. This view was taken on a wet 10 October 1964.

SALTCOATS Between May and November 1948 Barrow-in-Furness Borough Transport purchased new ten all-Crossley DD42/5s and ten all-Crossley DD42/4s. Clyde Coast Services Ltd purchased two of the DD42/5s in February 1957, and both were withdrawn in May 1962; it also purchased three of the DD42/4s in September 1958, and one of those, EO 8795, is seen at the same location; it would be sold for scrap in October 1967. The DD42/5 was 7ft 6in wide, whereas the DD42/4 was 8 feet wide.

MILLPORT The Isle of Cumbrae, also known as Great Cumbrae, lies just off the Ayrshire coast, a short ferry trip from Largs. It is 4 miles long and 2 miles wide. This is SJ 1315, a Scottish Aviation-bodied Commer Q4 that was new to Morrison of Millport, trading as Millport Motors, in June 1950. The bus had large scrolled 'Millport Motors Ltd' lettering on the rear, and the livery was red and cream. The location is, I think, Keppel Pier, which was the calling point for Clyde steamers on long-distance day excursions. mainly to Arran and Campbeltown. The Commers would ferry intending passengers to and from the town to connect with these excursions.

ISLE OF ARRAN Awaiting ferry passengers on 31 May 1963 is Weir's CSD 178, another Scottish Aviation-bodied Commer Q4 new in 1948. The Weir's of Machrie fleet also included a smart Bedford OB of 1949, DBN 627, and another Commer, GUS 129. Round-the-island tours for 7s 6d were the mainstay of many of the local coach operators; they proceeded in an anti-clockwise direction, this reducing the need for buses to pass each other in difficult places. From Brodick the coast road goes northwards, passing almost in the shadow of Goat Fell, through Corrie and into Glen Sannox. Through Glen Chalmadale the road drops to Lochranza, then turns south through Pirnmill, Machrie and Blackwaterfoot. The route continues south-east through Sliddery and Kildonan, then northward to Whiting Bay and Lamlash to complete the 56-mile circuit.

Above: **ISLE OF ARRAN** Brockhouse was a Scottish bodybuilder with premises at Livingstone Street, Clydebank, and entered the bus body business seriously in 1947, constructing a batch of coaches for Walter Alexander. The company built a new factory on the site to accommodate double-deck bodywork, but the venture did not become established due to the lack of skilled labour. However, it continued to build bus bodywork, with the majority of orders coming from Scottish operators, until 1951. New to A1 in August 1949 was this Brockhouse-bodied Foden PVSC6, CSD 711, seen here on the same day as the previous picture in the fleet of Lennox on the Isle of Arran.

Above right: **LOCHGILPHEAD** On the right is GUS 412, a Park Royal-bodied Maudslay Marathon 3 that was new to MacBrayne in 1949, seen here on 5 May 1964 under the ownership of Stag Garage Limited of Lochgilphead, which purchased the bus in October 1963. It would later pass to MacDonald & MacLennan of Lochgilphead in May 1966 and was withdrawn from service in October of that year. What makes this view interesting, and rare, is that MacBrayne's GUS 930, on the left, was also a Park Royal-bodied Maudslay Marathon 3 new in 1949, but in 1959 it had received new Duple bodywork; withdrawn in June 1968, the bus passed to a building contractor in Fort William.

Left: **CAMPBELTOWN** This is West Coast Motors SB 8500, a Burlingham-bodied Leyland PSU1/13 new in 1951 and photographed on 23 June 1963. This bus was first used on the West Coast service to Southend, at the foot of Kintyre, then was used regularly on the Lochgilphead to Campbeltown service. In my opinion this was one of the best ever coach designs.

Below: **SOUTHEND** lies 8 miles south of Campbeltown and is reputed to be where St Columba first set foot in Scotland. Working the Southend service of West Coast Motors on 24 June 1963 is SB 9281, a Duple-bodied Bedford SB new to Gold Line of Dunoon in 1953.

Left: **TARBERT** West Coast Motors, based in Campbeltown, Argyll, privately owned by the Craig family, commenced operations for passenger carrying in 1920, and a regular bus service between Campbeltown and Tarbert began the following year. New to Gold Line of Dunoon in 1959 was this Duple-bodied Bedford SB1, ESB 60, which was purchased by West Coast Motors and is seen here working the Campbeltown to Tarbert service on 8 September 1964.

The No 1 single on this day was You Really Got Me by the Kinks.

MACHRIHANISH In August 1923 the Post Office invited tenders for a new mail contract between Campbeltown and Tarbert, and to the surprise of Craig's (West Coast Motors) the contract was awarded to A. & P. McConnachie. The mail contract later passed to West Coast in 1930, while West Coast passed the Machrihanish service to McConnachie. The latter company purchased its first double-decker in 1960; KOD 585 was a Weymann-bodied AEC Regent III, with a 9.6-litre engine and Wilson pre-selector gearbox, which had been new to Devon General in 1949. The bus made the 600-mile-plus journey north uneventfully and remained in Kintyre until 1967, when it made the return journey south to be a part of the West of England Transport collection in Exeter. This view of KOD 585 on the Machrihanish service was taken on the same day as the previous one.

BALLOCH bus stance was near the railway station and, apart from the Glasgow routes, was also a start/end point for more local services to Helensburgh and Luss. Private coaches on day outings, or even just stopovers for a couple of hours, would park up in the same tarmac area, whose only facility was public toilets. Soon to depart for Luss on 1 July 1963 is No L442 (FVA 546) an NCME-bodied Leyland PD2/1 new in 1951; it would pass to Northern Roadways in August 1968.

Right: **WISHAW** From 1960 Hutchison of Overtown standardised on AEC Reliance buses, and in June 1963 acquired 327 NMP, with a Park Royal body, from A.C.V. Sales Limited, Southall; the bus had been a demonstrator with A.C.V. from new in March 1963. This view was taken on 12 October 1963, and the bus would be sold in 1968 to Robinson of Portrush in Northern Ireland.

Left: **EN ROUTE TO GLASGOW** Picking up a healthy load of passengers on 21 September 1963 is Central SMT No HR1 (XVA 444), an MCCW-bodied Leyland PDR1/1 new to J. Laurie & Company (Chieftain) of Hamilton in 1960; a total of 31 buses passed to Central on 1 October 1961 when Chieftain was acquired. This bus would pass to Graham's Bus Services of Paisley in April 1969.

Born on this day in Glasgow was Angus Macfadyen, best known for his role as Robert the Bruce in Mel Gibson's Braveheart.

Above: **NEAR MOTHERWELL** This view of Central SMT No H45 (FVD 745), a Guy Arab III with Guy bodywork, was taken on 1 February 1963; the bus was withdrawn and sold for scrap in July 1966. Behind it is No B16 (GM 7016), an ECW-bodied Bristol LD6G new in 1955. Due to the severity of the 1962-63 winter National Hunt racing was badly affected with 94 meetings cancelled during the freeze; there was just one meeting at Ayr in Scotland on 5 January 1963. The thaw began on 6 March 1963, the first morning of the year without any frost anywhere in the UK.

Photo **DESTINATIONS**

Strathclyde and South West Scotland (continued)

94	**LANARK**
95	**LANARK**
96	**ARDROSSAN**
97	**KILWINNING**
98	**AYR**
99	**DUMFRIES**
100	**THORNHILL**

Below: **LANARK** Central's Limited Stop services from Biggar and Peebles to Glasgow also called in at Lanark. Seen on 30 October 1963, on a short-working duplicate to the 244 service, is elderly Leyland No L288 (CVD 488), an NCME-bodied Leyland PD1A; it would pass to a dealer for scrap the following year. Also visible on the left is ECW-bodied Bristol LD6G No B25 (GM 7020), new in 1955, which later would pass to Highland Omnibuses in October 1969. Partially obscured by L288, by the taxi rank, is one of the ECW-bodied Bristol LS6Gs new to SMT in 1954.

Top left: **ARDROSSAN** This view was taken on 11 December 1964, the month after James McKinnon, one of the Ayrshire Bus Owners (A1 Service) Ltd, had taken delivery of two Park Royal-bodied AEC Renowns (ASD 890B and ASD 891B). Distinguishing features of McKinnon's buses were the white roof and the triangular-shaped destination screen.

Centre left: **LANARK** Guy, the Wolverhampton manufacturer, developed an underfloor-engined version of its Arab brand, the UF, and in 1952 Walter Alexander introduced the stylish Coronation body for this chassis. Like most of the other nationalised Scottish companies, Central placed an initial order for ten of these modern-looking and handsome vehicles, with 41-seat coach bodies with a central single-door entrance. They were allocated fleet numbers K35 to K44, the 'K' being the company's code for Guy single-deckers. Less than two years later Central SMT ordered ten more with bus bodies, and these featured traditional cut-away rear entrances for stage-carriage use with a manually operated folding door for some kind of weather protection; these were given fleet numbers K45 to K54 (GM 5945 to 5954), and were allocated mainly between Hamilton and Carluke depots, and used on Hamilton locals and Carluke and Lanark area services. In Lanark on 30 October 1963 is No K45 (GM 5945), which was the first to be withdrawn from service in 1965 and passed to Alexander Fife for spares.

Born on this day in Glasgow was Justin Currie, best known for being a founder member of the band Del Amitri.

Bottom left: **KILWINNING** In November 1944 Glasgow Corporation took delivery of No 67 (DUS 424), an NCME-bodied Guy Arab II. However, it had a very short service life with the Corporation fleet and in 1952 passed to AA Motor Services Ltd's owning member Dodds of Troon. It received the ECW body from Guy Arab II XS 5564 in December 1961 and entered service in that month as No DT14, later being sold to a builder in Irvine in June 1967. This photograph was taken on 30 May 1964. Note the car on the right, a 1964 Hillman Imp, an early example produced by the Linwood factory in Renfrewshire.

Above: **AYR** Working a local Ayr service to the Burns Monument on 1 August 1964 is Western SMT No AL 615 (CSD 21), an Alexander coach-bodied Leyland PS1 new in 1949. It would be sold to a contractor in Middlesbrough in March 1966, and had passed to McKean of Glasgow by September 1967.

On this day, born just up the road in Irvine, was Scottish politician Fiona Hyslop.

DUMFRIES At the Dumfries depot of Western Scottish on 3 August 1964 is, on the left, No B 915 (8915 SF), one of six Alexander coach-bodied AEC Reliances purchased between June and August 1963 for the Edinburgh to London service and fitted with toilet accommodation. By comparison, on the right is Western SMT No 1839 (VCS 393), an Alexander coach-bodied Leyland PSU3/3R new in 1963.

Just a few weeks later, on 29 October, the Animals were in concert at the Lyceum Ballroom in Dumfries.

1964
Happenings (3)

August
Viet Cong gunboats attack US destroyers in Gulf of
     Tonkin
Last hanging takes place in Britain

September
Forth Road Bridge opens over Firth of Forth
In Jacksonville, Florida, John Lennon announces that
     Beatles will not play to segregated audience
Daily Herald ceases publication, replaced by *The Sun*
Malta obtains independence from Britain

October
Dr Robert Moog demonstrates prototype Moog
     synthesiser
Shinkansen high-speed rail system, world's first such
     system, inaugurated in Japan
Summer Olympics held in Tokyo.
Dr Martin Luther King Jr becomes youngest
     recipient of Nobel Peace Prize
Khrushchev deposed as leader of Soviet Union
     replaced by Leonid Brezhnev and Alexei Kosygin
Labour Party wins General Election; Harold Wilson
     is new Prime Minister
Northern Rhodesia becomes independent Republic
     of Zambia

November
Parliament votes to abolish death penalty for
     murder in Britain.
Verrazano Narrows Bridge across New York
     Bay opens as world's longest suspension bridge
NASA launches Mariner 4 space probe towards
     Mars

December
Sam Cooke, African-American singer and songwriter,
    shot dead in Los Angeles motel
Che Guevara addresses UN General Assembly
Kenya becomes a republic, with Jomo Kenyatta as
    first President
Wonderful Radio London becomes UK's
    fourth pirate radio station

THORNHILL Heading for Dumfries on 2 April 1963, possibly at Thornhill, is Alexander-bodied Leyland No L174 (AAG 113).

Index of operators and vehicles

A1 Service: ASD 890B 60
AA Motor Services: DUS 424 60
Aberdeen: BRG 935, BRS 30 9; BRS 527 10; GRG 186, KRG 241 12; KRS 260 13
Alexander Greyhound, T. D.: NHA 580 19

BOAC: RAG 652 44

Central: DVD 296 42; FGM 19 44; XVA 444, FVD 745; CVD 488 60 59; GM 5945 60
Clyde Coast Services: XKT 784, EO 8795 54

Dundee: YJ 9635 14; AYJ 368 15; EYS 962 16; JXC 218, AYJ 888 17; YJ 9136 18

Edinburgh: 747 EUS 22; DWS 352, DWS 845 23; GSC 236 24; GSF 660, GSF 697, JSF 145 25; OFS 962 26; No 998, VSC 80 27

Fife: BMS 859, KWG 585 20; 7407 SP, CST 5, MMS 741 21; GMS 413 24; FWG 838 39; GWG 274 43

Garner's: ECK 148 52

Glasgow: RMS 690, FYS 765 30; FYS 772 31; FYS 995 32; FYS 791, FYS 780 33; FYS 708 34; FYS 716 35; FYS 813, FYS 856 36; FYS 800 37; SGD 730 38; FYS 683, FYS 494 39; SGD 321 46; SGD 400 47

Highland Transport: HGC 148 3; BST 325 5; NSG 780 6; EST 392, ESC 452 7
Hutchison: 327 NNP 59

Lennox: CSD 711 56

McConnachie, A. & P.: KOD 585 58
McGill's: EHS 113 48; VKV 99, NHS 764, OHS 979 49
McLennan, A. & C.: EES 468, GDK 301 18
Midland: VWG 386 4; SVD 113, VWG 369 29; BMS 107 40; BWG 573 41; CMS 383 42; JMS 389 44; WG 9980, GWG 477 48
Millport Motors: SJ 1315 55

Northern: EAV 459, BWG 104 8; DSA 113 10

Scottish Omnibuses: DSG 176 23; FMS 983 24; KWG 569 26; PVD 567 26; ESC 422 27; SS 8015, 9961 SF, 480 DVA 28; BMS 110 29
Stag Garage: GUS 412 56
Strachans: FAV 333, GCA 54, SUG 7 11

Weir's: CSD 178 55
West Coast Motors: ESB 60 56; SB 8500, SB 9281 57
Western: AAG 101B 44; VCS 432 45; BSD 289 50; ESD 217 51; TCS 151 52; CSD 21 61; 8915 SF, VCS 393 62; AAG 113 63

Further reading on road transport from *The NOSTALGIA Collection*

Available while stocks last through all good booksellers